The Existentialist Cookbook

Also by Shawnte Orion

The Infernal Gaze, Red Booth Review

The Existentialist Cookbook

Poems

Shawnte Orion

The New York Quarterly Foundation, Inc.
New York, New York

NYQ Books™ is an imprint of The New York Quarterly Foundation, Inc.

The New York Quarterly Foundation, Inc.
P. O. Box 2015
Old Chelsea Station
New York, NY 10113

www.nyq.org

Copyright © 2014 by Shawnte Orion

First Edition

Set in New Baskerville

Layout and Design by Raymond P. Hammond

Cover Illustration:
"Slippery", 18" x 24" oil on masonite
by Carol Roque, 2013 | www.carolroque.com

Library of Congress Control Number: 2014945815

ISBN: 978-1-935520-92-4

The Existentialist Cookbook

Contents

Oven

Hymn Latte *13*
Weathered *14*
Unheard Symphony *15*
Notes from a Kurosawa Film Festival *16*
Om Sweet Om *18*
The Geometry of Truth *19*
Cheese *20*
Recycling Pangaea *21*
Beyond Translation *22*
Series of Concentric Stanzas *23*
Dreams *pl. n.* *24*
Kentucky Freud Chicken *25*
Things that Make Me Cry *26*
The Existential Chef *27*

Cupboard

Oncoming Traffic *31*
Cocoon *32*
Gravesite Reservations *33*
The Abortionist's Garden *34*
Do Androids Dream of Electronically-Deposited
   Unemployment Checks? *35*
Mallville *36*
Aladdin Theater, 11/30/1993 *37*
Shelved Before Kindled *38*
Sand Witch Craft *40*
iKu *41*
Avoiding Aphids *43*
Colors Stored For Never *44*
The Infernal Gaze *45*

Microwave

Barracuda *49*
Project Runway: Blacklight Challenge *51*
Unable to Surface for Air During Shark Week *52*
Of Doves & Olive Branches *53*
The Amazing Technicolor Dream Poem *54*
You're Living All Over Me Living All Over You *56*
Found Poem from a Television Interview with
  Chris Cornell as Soundgarden Exits the
  1992 PinkPop Festival Stage *57*
Ash to Ash to Dust to Stone *58*
Edgar Allan Poe Elegy Delivered By Basho *60*
Breaking Dawn Within A Dawn Haibun *61*
(in jest) lowercase *62*
Sincerest Form of Rejection *63*

Neighbor's Sugar

Stray Dawn *67*
Love in the Time of Hand-Sanitizer *68*
Eight-Proof Path to Enlightenment *69*
Poem Yet To Be Written By David Chorlton *70*
Poem Yet To Be Written By Bill Campana *71*
Beached *72*
Male Pattern Breakfast *73*
Dogma *74*
Facsimile *75*

vii

Irreversible   *79*
Papercuts   *80*
Continental Breakfast   *81*
Sleeveless   *82*
Ink   *83*
Love Poem #9   *84*
Still Life with Sticky Rice   *85*
The Entomologist's Valentine   *86*
Breakfast Shaped Smacks of First Light   *87*
Upon Impact   *88*
Dedication   *89*

for Kimmey,
Zerrick and Josette

Oven

Hymn Latte

Though I've never acquired its taste
I pray to coffee as others
pray to god. *Please grant me the strength*

to endure this eight-hour shift. To stay awake
late enough to experience
a night worth regretting.

Please don't let me doze behind the wheel
during the drive home lullaby
or nod off during conversation.

Though I've never acquired its bitter taste
so I can only swallow that hallowed caffeine
diluted in cocoa or caramel.

But I still believe. I know you're there
listening to my prayers
beneath clouds of whipped cream,

steamed milk, dogma and hazelnut.
Dark Roast gospel translated from Irish Cream
into French Vanilla. Sacred scones

baptized in espresso. Holy mochaccino
shrouded in sugar. Foam faith
blessed with cinnamon. Amen.

Weathered

The wind looks for morning
fog, kites and stripes
dangling from a flagpole.

But finds the tumbleweed on the side of the road.
Finds poorly fitting hats and worse
fitting toupees. Finds your homework papers
spread across the picnic table and the ten dollar bill
among the leaves on the sidewalk.

The wind looks for sailboats, but finds
each miniscule opening
between the buttons of your
brand new jacket.

Unheard Symphony

Eyes closed, I exist
only as a vibration
in a world of pure sound.

Pervading the cosmos, finite tones
resonate throughout space
echoing into infinity.

Removing the mystery from coincidence
frequencies blend and absorb each other
harmonizing into a universal key.

Opening my eyes, I will
trust in this noise, even
if they call it God.

Notes from a Kurosawa Film Festival

Rationed bowls of rice
turn seven ronin into seven
samurai if they
hunger for nourishment
or honor

Isolated arrows are easily
broken across the knee
but arrows bundled
together in your quiver
remain stronger than family

Seeing a stray dog
run away with a severed
hand in its mouth
indicates that you have wandered
into a very bad part of town
unless you are a hungry dog

Shakespeare could have been a samurai
who was a samurai in a former life

Young boys caught
sneaking through the forest
for a glimpse of the foxes'
secret wedding procession
find it neither as forbidden
nor as fascinating
as a glimpse of the foxes'
secret honeymoon night
but are still condemned
to commit seppuku

Acting terrified for the camera
becomes more convincing
if none of the arrows
flying past your head
are fake arrows

Shelter from the storm
is always found
beneath the Rashomon gate
but truth is left
shivering in the rain

No one will hear you hum
your own late night elegy
if your dying moments are spent
alone on a swingset in the snow
but you will be forever
remembered by the schoolchildren
who find your cold
body in the morning

Om Sweet Om

This house is never more silent
or still than before morning.

Only amplifying the noise
of a rambunctious kitten. Too lost

in the Zen of her moment
to be annoyed or distracted

by me. Trying
to meditate on the sofa.

The Geometry of Truth

They pretend that graphing
polar extremes enables the truth
to be plotted as a coordinate
exactly halfway between.
But truth can not be balanced.
Truth is not a linear equation.

Truth is removed from that meridian.
A triangle. Not isosceles.
Not resulting from two congruous angles,
two balanced sides.

It might be evident and obtuse, but often
truth is dangerously acute. Sharp enough
to slice misconceptions or wrists.

The truth is never equilateral.
Truth is scalene with mismatched angles
uneven sides. Sides occasionally so distant
that their hypotenuse can only hint
at that Pythagorean reality.

Cheese

Before science finally proved
what the moon was truly made of,
any waitress would warn you

that the moon is not for vegans.
Who do not care how evenly the moon
melts across brick oven pizza.

Who have no appreciation
for how perfectly a subtle taste of moon
compliments a glass of Chardonnay.

Preferring alternative soy-based
satellite substitutes like Titan and Europa.
Vegans whose mouths have never salivated

over the thought of a curdled moon
aging to perfection
beneath its mouldy cratered rind.

Vegans who denounce the moon
as heaven's fondue pot and refuse to stir it
even if they are holding the big dipper.

Recycling Pangaea

Refusing to go green
I no longer carry cash
never fold paper dollars
into cotton pockets
so the next two-liter
bottles of cola I carry
home from the convenience
store in plastic bags
will be purchased with a debit card
from my nylon wallet

Somewhere in the Pacific
ocean currents converge
swirling stray litter
into a vortex of trash
a plastic island
floating puzzle piece
bigger than Texas

No longer thirsty
but I keep drinking Evian
hoping the next
empty bottle I toss
completes the polystyrene
super continent
finally unifying
Seattle and Tokyo

Beyond Translation

There was no blue
in ancient Greece
Homer's skies were iron
and bronze and they hung
above a wine-dark sea

Likewise *chloros*
seemed to be the word for green
but in literature of the time
honey was chloros
dew was chloros
even tears and blood

As if the blood's red hue
was less important than whether
it was fresh as morning dew
moist as honeyed tears
or still as an afternoon

Series of Concentric Stanzas

Bumble bee gathers
pollen for its queen
from the heart of an orchid's bloom

Puddle reflects
sun buried in clouds
through a floating cluster of leaves

Isle absorbs
endless lashing of waves
sent from surrounding tides

Trees hush
still in the fleeting
repose of the hurricane's eye

Dreams collapse
on the floor of my mind
after the dance of last night's sleep

Dreams *pl. n.*

Mysterious river
connecting
lake and sea

you lie on the embankment
eyes closed
plunging hand into stream
grasping at powerful currents
water flowing between your fingers
rushing toward the sea

you stand
empty handed
but notice your hand still wet
water dripping from each finger
as the Sun dries your arm

Kentucky Freud Chicken

Do you subconsciously desire
a taste of your Mother's
thigh or breast meat?

Would you like your soda Id
Ego or Super Ego sized?

Original Recipe Transference:
I bear resemblance to your dead Father
so you are only ordering a vanilla milkshake
because you think I want you
to order a vanilla milkshake.

Would you like a side order of cocaine?

Potatoes are mashed and repressed
with Rorschach splatters of gravy.

I assume you meant coleslaw
when you asked if the meal
comes with cold sore. Porn-on-the-cob
was a similar slip of the tongue.

Eleven herbs and childhood traumas:
You only demand to speak to my manager
because of your hatred for your Father.

Greasy buckets of buffalo hot wings
represent your flightless dreams.
Your inability to escape.

I do want you to order a vanilla milkshake
so I can watch your puckered mouth
struggle to suckle sips
through the end of a straw. A tiny
inadequate straw.

Things that Make Me Cry

You
slicing onions
in our new kitchen

In our old kitchen
slicing onions
by myself

The Existential Chef

Never grocery shops on an empty stomach
but always knows exactly what to cook
for the diner who has already eaten nothing.

Insists that every meal is only an appetizer
for the next meal, because fleeting attempts
to satiate hunger are futile.
But preps the kitchen, anyway.

Washes his hands, so they will be
ready to get dirty. Wears an apron
to protect his clothing from stains
and another apron to protect the first.
Understands that no colander can strain
meaning from this life.

The existential chef only uses
three types of fruit: fruit that is almost ripe,
fruit that is ripe and fruit that used
to be ripe. Stares into the pot
left upon a scalding stove
just to prove nothing
delays its water from boiling.

Has learned that perfectly roasted lamb
becomes tender enough to slice like butter.
Olive oil drizzled over baked potatoes
tastes like butter and Gruyère cheese
sprinkled into a heated skillet melts
just like butter, but what remains
most like butter is butter.

Uses malaise as a secret ingredient.
Garnishes every plate with ennui.
Only uses two types of vegetables:

vegetables that are rotten
and vegetables that are not
rotten, yet. Cooks lunch
knowing that by dinnertime
you will only be hungry again.

The existential chef is uncertain
which course got served first-
the chicken cacciatore or the omelet.
Scoffs at egg-timers for only
measuring the amount of nows
betweens nows.

Believes life should be sautéed
directly over the flame with fresh herbs
and lemon zest, while death simmers on low
toward the back of the stove.

Allows yesterday to marinade
in sweet and sour memories. Prefers today
peeled and eaten raw, but owns no Tupperware
for preserving leftovers because tomorrow
should never be taken for granted.

Cupboard

Oncoming Traffic

No therapist's couch
provokes more introspection
than a freeway late at night

car keys taking you
further than bottles
of prescription pills

headlights illuminating
only the road ahead
emphasizing focus and clarity

full throttle acceleration
reminding you that even
in the rearview mirror

objects of affliction
are closer than remembered

Cocoon

Snow covers the windowsill and frosts the panes.
Obscuring the view of the street where hapless drones
march to and from thankless occupations.

        I sip hot tea
        from an old chair
        near the fireplace

Sleek automobiles line the freeway. Burning gasoline that pays
for a distant war that will orphan an unborn daughter.

        I close my eyes
        so I can hear the faint music
        echo from another room

Smoke rises from glowing chimneys to sway like charmed
serpents and darken the haze that dims my view of the night stars.

        I feel myself turn
        and revolve with the other planets
        around an oblivious sun

Gravesite Reservations

They are digging more graves
for people condemned
by implied allegiances

and perceived associations.
They are digging more graves
but I ask no one to kill or die

for me. They are digging
more graves but I want
everyone to be united

through division. Dissolving
philosophical, political
and religious affiliations.

They are digging more graves
but I want to give everyone
their own shovel.

The Abortionist's Garden

Neighbors kept such vivid gardens
praising the glory of life, through roses
and hyacinths whose every bloom
consummated the embrace
of sun and earth.

She only ever watered
in the dark of night.
A suspicious assortment of plantings
that always seemed peculiar
in spite of the familiar scent of Sage
Parsley and Ginger.

But Tansy, Pennyroyal, Savin
Artemisia and Queen Anne's Lace
would cause the bleeding
that can make a miscarriage of an abortion.

Leaving Black Cohosh and Evening
Primrose to temper the womb,
until Angelica or Cotton Root Bark
force enough contractions
to exile the unwelcome embryo.

Do Androids Dream of Electronically-Deposited Unemployment Checks?

Job security
isn't manufactured
on this assembly line.

It might sound technical
but I basically press
buttons on a machine

while they invent a machine
to press the buttons
on my machine and I can only

hope this new machine
will have its own buttons
that also need to be pressed.

Mallville

With his kindergarten haircut
and conspicuous plastic eyeglasses
obscuring the geometry of his cheekbones
through non-prescription lenses,
Clark Kent is a super hipster.

Grew up in Kansas but he was born
someplace else. You've probably never been there.
He liked the design on his chest
before it became the letter S.
Back when it was just symbolic.

Faster than an Instagram upload.
More powerful than a Thursday afternoon hangover.
Able to leap to conclusions in a single snark.
But downplays all abilities and superpowers
so you can't tell if he's underachieving.
Uses supersonic hearing to listen to unsigned
garage bands Pitchfork's never heard of.
X-ray vision framed by plastic
non-prescription eyeglasses.
The Man of Irony has a weakness
for radiant minerals and a fetish for capes.
Thinks Green Lantern sold out.

Doesn't rely on fossil fuels. His mode
of transportation leaves no carbon footprint.
Built his fortress of solitude
completely off grid. Still romanticizes newsprint.
Prefers steampunk technology. The Man of Iron Alloy
ignores your Skype and text message
pleas for help, unless he stumbles
upon a vintage phone booth.

Aladdin Theater, 11/30/1993

You mentioned Vonnegut
in several magazine interviews
so I flung a paperback copy
of Galápagos toward the stage
lost my balance and fell
from the seats where I stood
watching that book
spin above the crowd.

Until it bowed to physics. Opening against
the resistance of the dark. Bursts of light
ricocheted from fluttering pages
as it dropped into the front row.

Stepping to the edge of the stage
you pointed toward the floor until someone
raised a novel to your hand. Lighting your face
like fluttering pages in a dark concert hall
before thumbing your way through chapters
for a few quotes to hurl
back into the crowd.

Shelved Before Kindled

autobiography: I collect more books
than I could ever read. My attention
is often diverted to new books
before finishing the last.

reference: books are divided
according to subject and arranged
alphabetically according to author.

biography: she borrows rare books
returning them with her own bookmarks
forgotten within the pages
of the final chapter.

mystery: a thick anthology leans
into the empty slot left behind
where a novella should be found.

horror: opening the old book with no title
at the end of the last shelf will release
captured souls of previous readers
trapped between
pages like revenant bookmarks.

self-help: even compulsive purchases
of books I have no intention of reading
infuse my subconscious
with new ideas and awareness
while neglected on a dusty shelf.

historical non-fiction: secondhand books
contain comments and annotations
scribbled into the margins
by former readers.

romance: the widow next door
watches me read French novels
in front of my bedroom window
without any curtains
without any shirt.

collected poems: rows of books
decorated with abandoned bookmarks
rising like headstones from middle pages
commemorate where my fleeting passions
were abruptly laid to rest.

fiction: someday I will return to these bookmarks
and resume reading from the point of interruption.

Sand Witch Craft

The only way
to convey how
long I waited
for this chicken
salad sandwich
to arrive at my
table is to keep
in mind that I
ordered an egg
salad sandwich.

iKu

happens in Vegas
stays in Vegas except that
syphilitic rash

failed intervention
mom addicted to Botox
raises no eyebrows

got married had kids
but she's stuck with that awful
tattoo forever

my adolescence
was a simile but felt
like a metaphor

Harry Potter's scar
inflicted in utero
coat hanger scratches

Twilight Beverly
Hills Nosfera210
Latter Day Anne Rice

bad babysitter
outside the lines with fifty
shades of Crayola

dropped long distance tryst
still hung up on telephone
sex operator

no one climaxes
and it makes no difference
existential porn

Tony the Tiger
on a drug called Frosted Flakes
with Charlie Sheen blood

Freud knows your husband's
huge rose bouquet compensates
for very small stem

jkLOL
omgLMAO
wtf

cellphone contact list
scrolls only same gender names
homotextual

value-belt chicken
drive-thru morality sized
nuggets before swine

blew self to bits but
would trade these damn virgins for
one bacon-wrapped whore

almost Googled porn
but left that for tomorrow
procrasturbation

Avoiding Aphids

Surrounded myself with silk plants
because I hate funerals
even for azaleas.

My failures camouflaged
by synthetic foliage that requires
no water, photosynthesizes nothing.
Never bends toward the sun.

Left in the corner of the room
to decorate my imitation of life
also rooted in Styrofoam soil.
My fake plastic world that never
needs to be re-potted
into a larger existence.

Colors Stored For Never

in memory of Mark Erickson

You heard the city ignore you. Deadlocked
procession of yawns. I try to ignore
missing you in the hush of fireworks.

A thimble of dreams. Crumpled origami
of birthday photographs. Don't exhale. Wind
quarantined in tires. I'm going to miss

ignoring you. Your mercury music
leaking from the car stereo. I wish
my drive to work was farther. I wish

nostalgia wasn't wasted on the mature.
Don't miss the exit. Don't pass
out in the backseat. Be my cross

country road trip. My flickering
halogen bulb. Not the cotton-tongued moth
plastered against the windshield.

The Infernal Gaze

I have stared into the mirror
until my face became completely
inhuman
a stranger to myself

I have repeated words
until reducing them to mere noise
a ridiculous pastiche of sound
that should never mean anything
to anyone

and then my world died around me

memories receded
into the vague meld of histories and myths
like the edge of the world
or the orbit of the sun

like whatever holds true today

Microwave

Barracuda

If Sarah Palin drowns
in an earmarked pet-project cauldron
filled with a mixture of freshly-drilled Arctic
National Wildlife Refuge oil and polar bear blood
then she was not a witch.

Even if it was real, Global Warming
could never thaw her heart.
She knows that you can put lipstick
on a seventeen year old girl
who has been deprived of comprehensive Sex
Education, but your NRA lobbyist
will only have nine months
to arrange the shotgun wedding.

Those go-go boots helped pray away my gay
and made the creationism of her bridge to nowhere
into a 398 million dollar catwalk -worth
every penny. She knows that if Alaskans
weren't meant to be pale, they would live
somewhere other than Alaska.
Someplace exposed to more than 5 hours of daylight
during winter months. So installing that tanning bed
in the Governor's office was a task from God.

John McCain is the only dinosaur she believes in.
She can see Uncle Ted's seven felony convictions
from her house. She knows that presidential elections
are glorified beauty pageants and not having
any answers for important questions
makes you a Maverick.

She understands and emphasizes Homeland Security.
Vows to protect America's prosperity
like a clever Yahoo e-mail password. She will fight
Alaskan Gray Wolves over there, chasing and shooting
them from the safety of helicopters
so we won't have to fight them over here.

And Sarah Palin knows that if books
weren't meant to be burned, they would be made
of something other than paper.
A flame-retardant material able to withstand
the friction of contradictory ideas, the heat
of dissent. She knows that if books weren't
meant to be burned, they would not contain
inflamatory ideas.

Project Runway: Blacklight Challenge

Phosphorescent ballet of needle
& thread. Ultraviolet motivation
fueled by fantasy. Neon mood.

Measures of proportioned tulle.
Gravitational lull. Quiet fabric
speaks to nobody.

Sleeveless dazzle of stardust.
made to work and upholstered
to glamorous execution.

Twirled into fluorescent
cape nebula. Love it
or look at the sun.

Unable to Surface for Air During Shark Week

Drowning in the Discovery Channel's wake,
from the comfort of my couch. Anchor
dragging through commercials.

Survivors recount sinking ships. Long nights
clinging to floating debris. Drifting four days
before spotted by rescue planes, but found
after only several hours, by swarms of whitetip
and tiger sharks. Others who panicked
were pulled beneath the tide by leg or foot.
Staining waves crimson.

Television turned off, I dive into bed.
Thankful that I would never know such fear.
Deep blue sheets up to my neck. Head floating
on a seafoam pillow. Swimming into sleep.
Dreams splashing in my ears. Until the kitten

notices my toes. Dangling like fins
over the edge of the bed.
Luring feline predators of the deep
to feet fragrant of catnip chum.
Poised to pounce as ankles twist
rolling blankets into waves. Row of claws
sharp as great white teeth
carve nightmares into my dreams.
Too far from shore
to be rescued before dawn.

Of Doves & Olive Branches

Noah's faith in God never wavered
when skeptics scoffed
at his claim that the Lord's voice
commanded him to whittle
a gigantic wooden raft and sign
a forty day lease
but he still must have felt
some nervous anxiety
about bringing two bark beetles
two woodpeckers and two termites
aboard that ark

The Amazing Technicolor Dream Poem

In chapter 37 of Genesis
Joseph reached the age of seventeen
before his eleven brothers
conspired to murder him
out of jealousy
for the coat of many colors
their father gave him as a gift.

Not because it signified that Joseph
was obviously Jacob's favored son
but because even the first
Tie-dye garment known to man
was tacky enough to provoke
immediate homicidal contempt and those
acid flashback hallucinations
he tried to pass off as prophetic dreams
only fanned the groovy flames of their hatred
sealing his own free-loving fate.

Now, Tie-dye is for anyone too indecisive
to settle on a favorite color. Tie-dye
convinced your parents that the most
individualistic and counterculture thing they could do
was to dress exactly like everyone else
who was trying to be different.

Tie-dye is far out, but even farther within.

Tie-dye is the reason Supreme Court Justices,
Hot Goth Girls and Batman wear black. Tie-dye
never gets invited to a royal wedding.
Tie-dye is the reason brides wear ivory.
Tie-dye has caused chameleons to spontaneously combust.

Tie-dye is responsible for high school dropouts
suddenly becoming passionate enough
about the intricacies of chemistry
to study and research how dye molecules
form covalent bonds to cellulose based fibers
such as cotton, wool and hemp by simply
raising the PH with a little sodium carbonate.

Tie-dye made The Beatles tune in, made Bob Dylan plug in
made Jimi Hendrix check out. Tie-dye is the reason
Johnny Cash wore black. Tie-dye is the hippie
rainbow deadheads follow to find
where that nine-fingered leprechaun
hid his pot of pot.

Tie-dye is for high school dropouts for whom
running a meth lab is just way too complicated.

You're Living All Over Me Living All Over You

Lou chewed like a cow.
Just random things.
Chew on them loudly.

Once on tour, I bought
this Cookie Monster doll.
I looked in the van and Lou was there
sucking on its eyeball.

I couldn't handle it. It was weird.
Disturbed me to my core. I think
I had to throw the thing out.

Found Poem from a J Mascis interview in Michael Azerrad's book
Our Band Could Be Your Life

Found Poem from a Television Interview with Chris Cornell as Soundgarden Exits the 1992 PinkPop Festival Stage

So loud. Like a little kid
spreading aggression with a really big toy.
So loud all over. Stage lights
coming from God. Is noise the wrong word?
So constantly loud.

I've tried. I wish I could. But musically,
I don't think I learned anything
from anyone else. Except there is one
similarity between a little kid from Seattle
spreading aggression with a really
big toy and Mr. Jimi Hendrix:
his parents live in Seattle and so
do mine. But it's so loud. No different
than putting lyrics over a soft song.

The audience is wet. The weather is awful.
Thunder and lightning. Just try
to make sounds people might not
hear the rest of the day.
The lightning was kind of cool.
But does it have to be so loud? Noise
is the perfect word.

Ash to Ash to Dust to Stone

Within the pages of a recent magazine interview,
Keith Richards finally admitted to snorting
a line of his dead father's ashes. Upon hearing
this news, Robert Downey Jr., Lindsay Lohan,
Pete Doherty and Kate Moss immediately
begged to have their fathers cremated.

Founding Stones guitarist Brian Jones
used to take his father's ashes swimming.
Charlie Watts uses two pencils
to tap on the urn that holds
his father's ashes and he's been tapping
the same damn beat for forty years.

Keith Richards had the audacity to charge $175
for a back-row balcony-seat glimpse
of his father's ashes during the first
of many farewell tours, although critics claim
that the ashes of Keith Richards' father are merely
evaporated leftovers of muddy waters and are kept
in the same old urn that was stolen
from the ashes of Howlin' Wolf's father.

The ashes of Keith Richards' father can't get
no satisfaction. They once sat on the Altamont stage
dumbfounded in the urn while Keith
launched into a guitar solo as the Hell's Angels
stabbed a man to death.

The ashes of Bill Wyman's father spend each night
inside a barely-legal urn. An urn so young
that it's often mistaken for his daughter's ashes.

Tina Turner knows that the ashes
of Mick Jagger's father have been laced
with brown sugar and are kept
in an urn that's painted, painted, painted.
Painted black. The ashes of Mick Jagger's father
have allegedly been mixed in the same urn
as the ashes of David Bowie's father
but no one will confirm or deny the rumor.

To this day, Mel Gibson's dad denies
that Keith Richards' father
was ever cremated in the first place.

Edgar Allan Poe Elegy Delivered By Basho

Married my cousin
our family tree sprouts new
branches nevermore

Poe pioneered both
modern short tale and fetal
alcohol syndrome

Confessed to murder
for delicious pink tell tale
conversation heart

The Bells bells the bells
the bells bells bells the bells bells
the bells bells bells bells

Lenore to Miss Clemm
Poe only pined for women
dead or underage

Poe's pre-teen cousin
nighttime visions are but wet
dream within wet dream

Watch at the border
for minutemen on your way
to Eldorado

Living happily
forevermore forced that damn
raven to eat crow

Breaking Dawn Within A Dawn Haibun

Edgar Allan Poe liked teenage girls. Edgar Allan Poe loved teenage girls. Enough to marry one of them. So Edgar Allan Poe knew teenage girls, in every biblical sense. But if he were himself a teenage girl, he would still be drawn to shadows. He would be a sullen Lolita who would rather hang out at the morgue than the mall. Prefer macabre to Maybelline. He would dye his hair raven-black. Paint his fingernails black-cat black. He would dress in varying shades of black. He would be the strange and unusual goth girlfriend you were afraid to break up with in high school. Renting Japanese horror films and listening to nothing but Bauhaus, while cutting himself. He would try to photograph ghosts and his whole life would be a dark room. One big dark room. He would be utterly alone and celebrate Halloween all year long. He would like monsters and werewolves. He might even love werewolves, but he would surely side with vampires, who despise sunlight for making them sparkle like golden scarabs. Whose souls are eternally damned. He would identify with beings forced to endure indefinite periods of isolation and value a vampire's willingness to happily wear the masque of the red death, during special cycles of the moon. He would cherish the fragrance of blood and become nauseous at the smell of wet-dog and Poe would appreciate the absence of a beating heart that might otherwise drive him to tell-tale insanity.

Nabokovian vampires
centuries-old means every
girl is underage

(in jest) lowercase

in Just-
recess   eddieandbill
play tetherball

while the lame   goat-footed
balloon man
whistles but maintains

a court-ordered   500 foot
distance   from the playground
fence

as a wee condition
of his parole

Sincerest Form of Rejection

Dear Anyjournal Review:

Thank you for the recent subscription offer.
I appreciated the opportunity to order
at a discounted rate.

Be assured that it has received careful
consideration and was reviewed with great interest. However,
I regret to inform you that it does not suit
my current reading needs,
so I must decide against subscribing.

Do not be discouraged. This rejection doesn't necessarily
reflect a lack of quality. You were close.
I receive hundreds of impressive
subscription offers each month and can only
subscribe to less than four percent of those publications.
Competition is keen. You were not close enough.

Please note that I do not wish to receive
further subscription offers from your publication
until at least eighteen months have passed.

If you are unfamiliar with my tastes,
you may want to order one of my chapbooks
or request a few sample poems with a self-addressed
stamped envelope to see the kind of work I prefer.

Unfortunately, the volume of offers I receive
prevents me from responding personally. Best of luck
in finding a subscriber elsewhere.

Neighbor's Sugar

Stray Dawn

Poem Yet To Be Written By Jack Evans

The night seemed to die
every morning
murdered by sunrise

Shadows left behind
commemorate each
previous night's mortality

Betraying the truth
that there is only one
everlasting night

Chased beyond the horizon
by daybreak but sneaking back
every time the sun turns its head

Like the stray cat who always
returns in the evening
looking for leftover

Scraps of dinner
only to find you three days
into a seven day fast

Love in the Time of Hand-Sanitizer

Poem Yet To Be Written By Rosemarie Dombrowski

Rubbing my palms together in scalding water
below the same faucet where you used to rub yours

reminds me of years of your bacteria
waltzing around the same drain's
porcelain dance floor as my own bacteria.

A tango of germs. Our pathogens cohabiting
in ways we never could.

Centripetal swirl of microbes; too minuscule
for the wandering eye, unless viewed
through the refraction of a lens.

Magnified and examined
our sterile relationship left in the petri dish
never mutated into a contagion
infectious as love.

Eight-Proof Path to Enlightenment

Poem Yet To Be Written By Dogo Barry Graham

Bringing light to a dark
corner of the bar
The Buddha sits patiently
waiting for the waitress to bring
another pitcher of beer.

All around him patrons are drinking
to their health, to their sorrows
drinking to their worldly attachments.

Exchanging miseries and failures
they can only express
when intoxicated.

But The Buddha is aware
that he is already drunk
he has always been drunk
and doesn't need
any alcohol to prove it.

Poem Yet To Be Written By David Chorlton

You step from the train greeted
only by the moon. Uncertain for a moment
whether you have arrived in Phoenix
or Vienna. You only know that the Kafka
paperback that accompanied you
for the past three hours has been forgotten,
left beneath your seat on the train
already leaving the station.

You imagine who might discover it
and wonder if they will begin
reading where you left off. You hope they appreciate
its well-worn pages and the powdery
desiccated wing of the Banded Sphinx
Moth that you were using as a bookmark.
You hope they agree with the significance
of the passages you carefully
underlined in red ink and you wonder
if they will take the book with them
once they reach their destination
or if they will also leave it
behind. Discarded for the next stranger
on his way to somewhere else.

Poem Yet To Be Written By Bill Campana

After opening a package of Ramen
I realized that I didn't have three extra minutes
so I ate that petrified brick of noodles
dry and crunchy and beige

Then I drank a glass of boiling water
burned my esophagus like a fuse
before sprinkling the mysterious
contents of the seasoning packet
onto a coffee table mirror

Chopped those granules
into parallel lines with a maxed out
credit card and snorted that MSG dust
through a rolled up food stamp

Then I did some jumping jacks

Beached

Poem Yet To Be Written By Cat Klotsche

I was perfectly happy
sinking into the depths of you

but tides pushed and pulled
waves rolled me toward the shore

abandoning me in the sand
with the other briny souvenirs

drying in the sun until
becoming so brittle that even

the lightest breeze could shatter
what used to be my shell

Male Pattern Breakfast

Poem Yet To Be Written By Aaron Johnson

First loves recede like hairlines
but your comb-over into my life
was like finding the perfect hat.
The one I wanted to wear
around all my old friends. Head held
high at the high school reunion.
Listening to everyone else
complain about their lives, their jobs,
their ex-husbands. Worrying about how
cold it would be in January.

But I just nodded knowing that my hat
would always keep me warm.

Warm like the pancake
on the bottom of the stack.
Waiting to melt your buttery kisses.
Bracing for your Aunt Jemima hugs.
There will be nothing but syrupy sweetness
inside our log cabin and when I walk outside
I no longer worry about the bitter winter air.
Unless whispers in the trees
blow into fierce shifting winds.

Dogma

Poem Yet To Be Written By Patrick Hare

A thorough investigation
revealed that the ruckus
outside my kitchen window
was being caused by two Jehovah's
Witnesses in the front yard.
Giving a meaty hambone
to my German Shepherd.

Not bound by Jehovah's commandments
I walked down the driveway and gave
them two lies:

how I deeply appreciated their generosity
because today was my dog's birthday.

Facsimile

Poem Yet To Be Written By Bakeem Lloyd

After accidentally transmitting
vocal vibrations in a magnetic field
from one place to another, Alexander Bell
could have never envisioned
weaving an entire world
of telecommunication threads
together in a fiber-optic tapestry.

Never envisioned technological
advancements enabling me to call
an ex-girlfriend at her mother's
apartment just to hang up on her
eleven times in a row or dialing
a stranger in the middle of the night
just to breathe heavily into her ear.

Never anticipated cordless phones
allowing me to pace between
rooms while waiting on hold.

Never predicted Caller ID
preventing me from ever again
having to answer calls
from debt collectors or mother-in-laws.

Never expected clandestine text messages
delivering lascivious flirtations
while sequestered in my cubicle.

Never foresaw grainy Zapruder-like
cellphone footage of you
flashing me from the sixth floor
window of the schoolbook depository
ambushed by a second texter

blowing me a kiss from the grassy knoll
knocking my head back
and to the left, back
and to the left.

Never expected this blanket of wi-fi
network coverage would leave me cold
leave me longing for the warmth
of a breakthrough invention like tin cans
tethered together by string
that would only let me
hear your voice.

Freezer

Irreversible

She lies still in the damp sand
staring into nowhere. Afternoon sun
warming her cold skin.

Rolling with the tide
waves guide her flaccid body
toward the quiet shore.

She falls into the sea
shattering her reflection
with a violent splash.

Pacing the guardrail
she worries about trimesters
in the morning light.

She lights a cigarette
walking toward the bridge
from the hotel where he said goodbye.

Alone in the car
she follows dark streets
lit only by the moon.

She carefully grabs her keys
trying not to wake
her husband from the couch.

Papercuts

You held her very last letter
above a flickering candle until
each word was devoured by flame.
Paper and memories incinerated.
Ash sinking into melted wax.
You leaned close. Lips puckered
like a kiss and blew that flame
away from the wick. Extinguishing
fragile light and heat. Banishing
shadows from surrounding walls.
Allowing wax to cool.
But opening that envelope
left a papercut impossible to ignore.
Hours and days pressing swollen flesh
to feel that nostalgic sting. Fingernails
digging beneath edges of scab
until it peels from the wound.
Preventing a clean heal
by exposing raw flesh and leaving
eternal scar tissue as a constant reminder
of fossilized memories
suppressed in hardened wax.

Continental Breakfast

Centered in panthalassic bed
we cuddled like Pangaea

on a lithospheric quilt.
Our big bang

spooned into one
supercontinent of exhaustion.

Sheet tectonics.
Rift of midnight tremors.

Seismic faults
dividing us by morning.

Bodies separated.
Drifting toward the bed's

opposite poles.

Sleeveless

I never noticed the difference
between naked and exposed
until your sweater was puddled on my floor
and your shoulders remained covered
in kaleidoscopic swirls of ink. A tattooed
cartography of memories and myths.
Sleeves I could never remove.

Ink

I wanted to write you a note this morning
leave it on your pillow
before I left for work
but I couldn't find my red pen

It would have said that you have no reason
to be jealous it would have been a proclamation
of loyalty it would have tried
to convince you of my devotion

But I couldn't find my red pen
and I could never scribble in this notebook
with any other hue

Love Poem #9

No one notices falling. Only the sudden
revelation of floor. The early-morning
arrival at a foreign destination
after sleeping through the journey.

No wonder potions were made
from boiled secretions of rare exotic frogs
left simmering for days. The frog
might have noticed falling

when dropped into the cauldron.
But soothing solace of lukewarm splash
mollified fears into tranquil complacency
as the temperature gradually increased

ever so slightly that the frog
remained calm and oblivious
to the scalding heat
until he was already cooked.

Still Life with Sticky Rice

Lack of depth
movement & algae

turns this plate of sushi
into a post-modern
aquarium where we
trawl for happy hours

fresh glances
reflected in slices
of the itamae's knife

tempura hand-rolls
pickled ginger
inside-out

poked
with chopsticks
but not
picked up

quivering sashimi
chilled to the raw

she smears
wasabi on my lips
insists there
isn't enough sake

in this world
or the next

The Entomologist's Valentine

They want you fluttering
above petals. Delicate
footprints left in pollen.

I want you sealed in a jar
under tightened lid. Exposed
from every lurid angle

behind clear glass. Forever-want
crystallized in your cocoon.

I want you pinned
to a slide and smoldering
beneath the microscope's lamp.

Or soaked in formaldehyde
to soften your thorax
for the scalpel's incision.

Breakfast Shaped Smacks of First Light

Now that her mornings are snooze
buttons of espresso & a borrowed
sweatshirt for the quiet

cab ride back to her apartment,
for the abbreviation of a shower,
before scrambling to the office,

she barely remembers Saturday cartoons
in footed pajamas. Loops & flakes of fructose.
Two scoops of marshmallow pebbles.

Fruitificial clusters of puffberries
& spoonfuls of bite-sized vitamin crisps.
A good source of bright colors

waiting to be dredged
from a bowl of skim milk
as frosted crunch turns soggy

with her empty hand
burrowing into the shiny
box of golden cardboard

until tiny fingers
discover someone else
already took the prize.

Upon Impact

We met by accident. Sudden collision
at the intersection of not-paying-attention
and running-red-light. My seat belt
held me back, while you
kissed shattered windshield.

For years you dug souvenir
slivers of dashboard
out of your shoulder. Shards of glass
embedded in your forehead
still surface
nine years down the road.

Our passengers
remain in critical condition
oblivious to the fragments of you
buried in my chest. Jagged shards
embedded far beneath my skin.

Dedication

Never sent you flowers
at the office. In case pollen
irritates your allergies
into asthma attacks.

Never bought you imported chocolates.
Knowing that one of my kisses
would not wake you
from diabetic coma.

Never threw midnight pebbles
at your bedroom window for fear
of shattering the glass and startling you
out of bed with bare feet.

Withheld many secrets
kept only to ensure
a reserve of fresh topics
should our conversations ever lull.

Acknowledgments

Grateful acknowledgment is made to the editors of the following publications, in which versions of some of these poems first appeared:

Barrelhouse: "Breaking Dawn Within A Dawn Haibun"
Canyon Voices: "Avoiding Aphids," "iKu," "The Amazing Technicolor Dream Poem," "Unable to Surface for Air During Shark Week," "Cheese," "Dedication,"
Crab Creek Review: "Things that Make Me Cry"
DASH Literary Journal: "Do Androids Dream of Electronically-Deposited Unemployment Checks?"
Feathertale Review: "Ash to Ash to Dust to Stone"
Fishbones Poetry Review: "Found Poem from a Television Interview with Chris Cornell"
Four Chambers Magazine: "Breakfast Shaped Smacks of First Light"
Garbanzo Literary Journal: "Of Doves & Olive Branches"
Gargoyle Magazine: "Colors Stored For Never"
Gloom Cupboard: "The Abortionist's Garden," "Ink"
In Our Own Words: A Generation Defining Itself Vol. 4: "Cocoon"
Juked: "Poem Yet To Be Written By Bill Campana"
Mason's Road: "Poem Yet To Be Written By David Chorlton"
Maelstrom: "Hymn Latte"
Merge: a journal of convergent ideas: "Barracuda," "Recycling Pangaea," "Irreversible"
Mouse Tales Press: "Stray Dawn," "Male Pattern Breakfast"
New York Quarterly: "The Geometry Of Truth"
No Alibi Press: "Gravesite Reservations"
Noctua Review: "Notes from a Kurosawa Film Festival," "Weathered"
Paper Darts Magazine: "Project Runway: Blacklight Challenge"

The Peralta Press: "Dreams pl. n."
Red Booth Review: "The Infernal Gaze"
Sakura Review: "Beyond Translation"
Stonecoast Review: "Shelved Before Kindled"
Suisun Valley Review: "Unheard Symphony"
The New: "Sincerest Form of Rejection"
Thin Air Magazine: "Kentucky Freud Chicken"
Up The River: "Love in the Time of Hand-Sanitizer,"
   "Eight-Proof Path to Enlightenment"

Special thanks to: my Caffeine Corridor Poetry Series co-hosts Jack Evans and Bill Campana; Rob Fix for all the guerilla camerawork; Rocky Yazzie for all the adventures and for dragging me to see Phoenix bands like Colorstore; Doug Bale for combining the words Kentucky and Freud into a title I couldn't resist; Charles Jensen for his Haibun workshop (and Hayden's Ferry Review for giving me a free pass to that Desert Nights Rising Stars writing conference); Scott Boras for assigning me the subject of Tie-dye for one of the Encyclopedia Shows at ASU; Four Chambers Press for bringing more literary life to the desert; Diane Lockward's prompt from The Crafty Poet which helped shape Sleeveless. David Nelson, Johnnie Clemens May, Kimberly Mathes and the rest of the Glendale Community College writing faculty for supporting all of my attempts to bring poetry to an audience and vice versa.

CPSIA information can be obtained
at www.ICGtesting.com
Printed in the USA
FFHW021648110319
50998733-56410FF